BATTLE OF
THE BULGE

by

Wallace B. Black
and
Jean F. Blashfield

CRESTWOOD HOUSE
New York

Maxwell Macmillan Canada
Toronto

Maxwell Macmillan International
New York Oxford Singapore Sydney

Library of Congress Cataloging-in-Publication Data

Black, Wallace B.
    Battle of the Bulge / by Wallace B. Black and Jean F. Blashfield. —
1st ed.
        p.   cm. — (World War II 50th anniversary series)
Includes index.
    Summary: Describes the events surrounding the German's last big offen-
sive to defeat and divide the Allied army and turn the course of the war in
late 1944.
    ISBN 0-89686-568-1
    1. Ardennes, Battle of the, 1944-1945 – Juvenile literature. [1. Ardennes,
Battle of the, 1944-1945. 2. World War, 1939-1945 – Campaigns.] I. Blashfield,
Jean F. II. Title. III. Series: Black, Wallace B.   World War II 50th anniversary.
D766.5.A7853   1993
940.54'214318—dc20

                                                              92-1722

Created and produced by B & B Publishing, Inc.

Picture Credits
Dave Conant (map) - page 15
National Archives - pages 3, 4, 6, 10, 12, 13, 16, 18, 19, 21, 22, 25, 26, 27, 29, 30, 31, 32, 33, 35, 38,
41, 43, 44, 45
United States Air Force - pages 9, 36

**CRESTWOOD
HOUSE**

Macmillan Publishing Company
866 Third Avenue
New York, NY 10022

Maxwell Macmillan Canada, Inc.
1200 Eglinton Avenue East
Suite 200
Don Mills, Ontario M3C 3N1

Macmillan Publishing Company is part of the Maxwell Communication Group of Companies.

Printed in the United States of America

First Edition

10 9 8 7 6 5 4 3 2 1

CONTENTS

1. One Bridge Too Far 5
2. The Road to the Ardennes 11
3. Watch on the Rhine 17
4. Battle of the Bulge 24
5. Bastogne Under Siege 30
6. Nordwind and Bodenplatte 34
7. The Bridge at Remagen 39
Glossary 46
Index 47

Chapter 1

ONE BRIDGE TOO FAR

Operation Overlord, the invasion of France by the Allied forces in World War II, began on D-Day, June 6, 1944. On that day 155,000 American, British and Canadian troops landed on Normandy beachheads. The goal of Overlord was to invade German-occupied France and land an army of 2 million men. The next goal was to invade Germany, defeat the German armies and force their surrender, thus ending World War II.

Overlord was successful and it was the beginning of the end for Adolf Hitler and the Nazi armies. But victory would not come easily. Germany had occupied almost all of western Europe since June of 1940. The battles on the ground and in the skies over Europe following Overlord continued until the unconditional surrender of Germany to the Allies on May 7, 1945.

The landings on the Normandy beaches were hard fought. Although the Allies had complete control of the skies and of the sea, German ground forces fought back fiercely. Casualties were high on both sides as U.S., British and Canadian armed forces strove to drive inland and advance toward Germany. However, short of supplies and fighting a huge, well-equipped German army, the Allied forces were tied down in Normandy for six weeks.

U.S. Army vehicles in a traffic jam in the snow-covered forests of the Ardennes. Much of the Battle of the Bulge was fought under such conditions.

Normandy Breakout

On July 25, with Operation Cobra, the breakout from Normandy began. The U.S. 3rd Army, commanded by General George S. Patton, broke through German defenses and drove deep into France to the south and west of Normandy. The British 21st Army Group, commanded by General Bernard Montgomery, surged east toward the Belgian border. The U.S. 1st Army, commanded by General Courtney Hodges, completed the breakout from Normandy and more Allied forces charged east and north toward the German border.

On August 15 Operation Dragoon landed Allied forces on the south coast of France. Free French and U.S. forces liberated Paris, the capital of France, on August 25. The German army was now fighting the Allies on three fronts—in Normandy, in southern France and in Russia.

In early September 1944 General Patton's 3rd Army, swinging eastward, reached the French city of Verdun only 60 miles from Germany. It appeared that the German army was in full retreat and that the Allies would be entering Germany within just a few weeks. But the Allied advances slowly came to a standstill.

Trucks of the Red-Ball Express were loaded at railyards and seaports in France and Belgium before forming high-speed convoys to deliver supplies to the front lines.

The problem of supplying the huge, fast-moving Allied forces was too great. Supply lines were stretched too far and Germans were fighting back fiercely. This led to ever-increasing shortages of fuel and other supplies. General Dwight D. Eisenhower, the supreme commander of the Allied forces, called a halt to the rapid advances and set about planning for the next course of action.

Red-Ball Express

The large quantities of supplies needed to support the huge Allied armies had to come through the French port at Cherbourg or in smaller amounts through temporary docks in Normandy. By mid-August the Allied forward lines were as much as 300 miles inland. The French railway system had been wrecked by Allied bombing and there were not enough trucks and transport aircraft available to carry the needed supplies.

To solve this problem, the Allies set up a high-speed trucking operation called the Red-Ball Express. This involved a fleet of some 6,000 trucks of all types driving at high speed on one-way roads in a giant loop to deliver the needed goods to several key points. During the first weeks of September they delivered more than 81,000 tons of supplies in just three weeks, but this was still not enough. And the Red-Ball Express itself consumed vast amounts of fuel and suffered severe maintenance problems.

There were now 2 million Allied troops in France spread along a 400-mile front from Switzerland on the south to the Netherlands on the north. This vast army needed to be supplied. New seaports closer to the front lines were needed but would not be opened until late November.

Eisenhower and Montgomery Clash

As time went by, the battered German armies began to regroup and fight back. Resistance to the Allied advances became stronger. With the approach of the fall season, bad weather began to be a problem. As supreme commander of the Allied forces in France, General Eisenhower favored a steady offensive along the entire German border, from Switzerland on the south to Belgium on the north. Slow, steady advances were being made except in the north along the Scheldt waterway and in the center of the Allied line in the Ardennes Forest of Belgium.

However, the British commander, newly appointed Field Marshal Bernard Montgomery, wanted to make a single concerted drive to the north through Belgium and Holland into Germany. It was his opinion that existing supply lines could not support operations along the entire front. He thought that if his plan was given full support, a successful campaign to the north would open up seaports at Antwerp in Belgium and Rotterdam in the Netherlands, providing the supplies the Allies needed. In Field Marshal Montgomery's opinion a successful northern campaign could end the war with Germany within a few months.

Operation Market-Garden

General Eisenhower finally gave in to Field Marshal Montgomery and approved the plan for Market-Garden, as the proposed operation was called. Action was slowed on other fronts to provide supplies for this offensive.

Market-Garden called for 10,000 airborne troops made up of British and Polish paratroop and glider forces to land near the key city of Arnhem, on the north side of the Lower Rhine River in the Netherlands. There they would secure the city and capture a railroad bridge, a pontoon bridge and the main highway bridge.

However, the British needed additional airborne troops to support the campaign. The U.S. 82nd and 101st Airborne Divisions were placed under Field Marshal Montgomery's command and were to capture other key bridges to the south of Arnhem. They landed 10,000 additional troops south of the Lower Rhine on the approach to Arnhem.

Canadian paratroopers for Operation Market-Garden landing near Arnhem in the Netherlands

These two missions were to prepare the way for a large British force, the XXXth Corps, to drive northward to Arnhem, driving defeated German forces before them. Allied forces advancing through the Netherlands could then bypass the northern end of the German West Wall (the Siegfried Line) which ended at the Netherlands border, and advance toward Berlin, the German capital.

British Airborne Forces Fail

The plan called for the British airborne units to capture Arnhem and its bridges in just two days. However, there were unforeseen delays and German forces learned of the British plans from captured documents. As the British paratroopers finally reached the railroad bridge, it was blown up by the Germans. The pontoon bridge had already been destroyed. One heroic British commander, Major John Dutton Frost, set up a defensive position in Arnhem and tried to capture the highway bridge, only to be repulsed by superior German forces. With fewer than 500 men, Frost held his position for three days waiting for reinforcements and air support that never arrived.

Opening the Scheldt Waterway

Admiral Sir Bertram Ramsay, the Allied naval commander in chief, and General Eisenhower had decided that the port of Antwerp in Belgium must be opened so that supplies in quantity could be delivered to the Allied armies. Antwerp is located at the eastern end of the Scheldt waterway about 50 miles inland from the North Sea. This huge port could handle the large ocean-going ships that would deliver the supplies and reinforcement needed. Although the Allies had captured Antwerp in early September, the Scheldt waterway was still controlled by the Germans. It had to be cleared.

Field Marshal Montgomery assigned the task of driving the German defenders from the Scheldt to the 1st Canadian Army. With heavy support from Allied naval and air force units, the Canadians began their attacks on October 1.

Attacking in force on both the north and the south sides of the Scheldt, they met stiff resistance. The lowlands surrounding the Scheldt were marshy and were flooded as dikes holding back the sea waters were bombed. Amphibious assaults were made on the northern shores of the

Allied troops cross a pontoon bridge as they pursue German troops in the battle for the Scheldt waterway.

Heavily armed American troops follow a tank down a forest roadway in the Huertgen Forest.

Scheldt to reinforce the Canadians. Finally after a month of hard fighting the German forces guarding the waterway were surrounded and forced to surrender. Fighting ended on November 8 but the waterway still had to be cleared of mines. The first ships loaded with the badly needed supplies did not arrive at Antwerp until November 28.

The Battle of the Huertgen Forest

Meanwhile during the months of October and November, fighting continued all up and down the German border. Two British armies continued the battles in the north, attempting to drive into the Netherlands and eastward toward the Ruhr Valley in Germany. Five U.S. armies pressed on toward Germany from Aachen on the north to the Swiss border on the south.

The main U.S. attacks in the north were directed at Aachen, Germany, an ancient, embattled city dating back to the time of Charlemagne in A.D. 800. General Courtney H. Hodge's 1st Army led the way. After three weeks of bitter fighting, Aachen's defenders retreated eastward, leaving the city in ruins and open to the advancing U.S. troops. It was the first German city to fall into American hands.

U.S. forces then continued to fight their way eastward into the Huertgen Forest. This 30-square-mile patch of heavy woods lies at the northeast corner of the Ardennes. It was packed with German defenses including tank traps, hidden machine gun nests, mines and barbed wire. Four U.S. divisions were sent into this death trap during October and November and all suffered terrible losses.

By December 1 the U.S. 1st Army, now supported by General William H. Simpson's 9th U.S. Army, had breached the German West Wall and were preparing to attack the Roer Valley to capture the large dams on the Roer River. But in reaching that goal, the four U.S. divisions battling their way through the Huertgen Forest had suffered more than 30,000 casualties, with over 10,000 dead in just two months. The German defenders suffered even heavier losses as they tried to hold back the assault on their country. Both sides suffered terribly from continuous combat in the wet, freezing weather.

A Dangerous Gap Between the Armies

As the battle of Huertgen Forest was being fought, General Patton's 3rd U.S. Army, 150 miles to the south, was battering away at the Maginot Line, the old French defense system that had failed to stop the German army in 1940. Now the Germans had turned the French guns westward to defend against the attacking Americans.

By December 4, General Patton's forces had begun to break through the West Wall into the heavily industrialized Saar region of Germany. General Simpson's 9th Army was loaned to Field Marshal Montgomery to continue the battles for control of the dams in the Roer Valley. On December 7, 1944, General Eisenhower reaffirmed his orders that the advance toward the Rhine River in Germany should be carried on along the entire front.

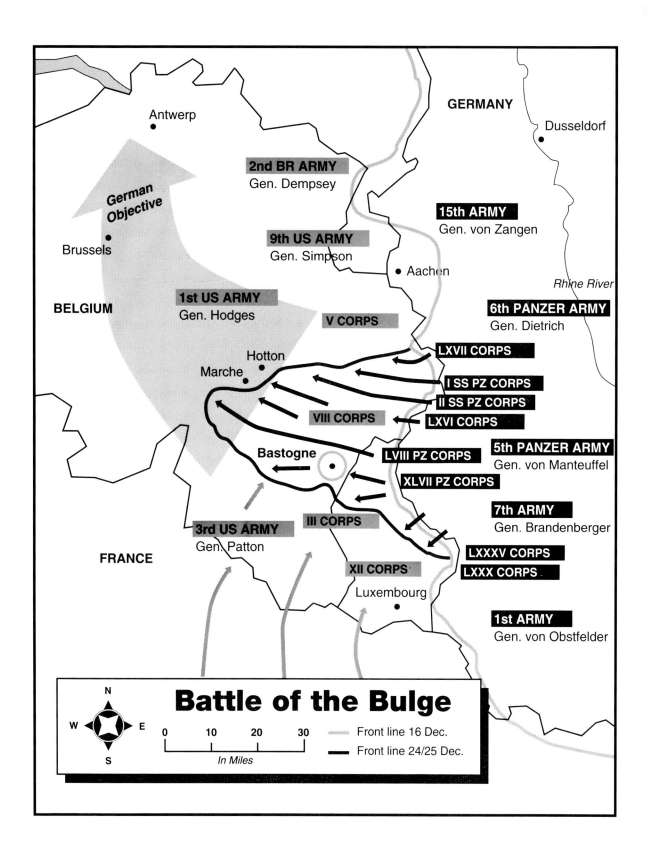

While the U.S. forces were advancing through Aachen into Germany and General Patton's forces were attacking the Maginot Line, a gap in the U.S. defenses occurred. As these two large armies were busy fighting they had left only one understaffed U.S. Army Corps to defend the huge Ardennes region. Along the rugged 85-mile-long border 83,000 U.S. troops in six divisions were thinly spread throughout the Ardennes Forest. Half were inexperienced units that had never seen battle. The other half, exhausted and worn out in battle, had been sent there to rest and to be re-equipped and reinforced. This lightly defended area was one that the Germans knew well and had every capability of attacking.

Meanwhile the German forces had been steadily reinforced and strengthened. Entire armies had been reorganized and rearmed. The Germans were fighting more fiercely as the Allies threatened their homeland. At the same time, with continuous combat and with supplies still arriving slowly, many U.S. units were battle weary, under-equipped and undermanned. It was a situation filled with danger, danger that the Allied high command failed to recognize. The poorly defended Ardennes was the weakest spot in the long Allied front.

This grim-looking and heavily armed German soldier was typical of the crack German troops preparing for the invasion of the Ardennes.

Chapter 3

WATCH ON THE RHINE

During the fall of 1944 most German generals were ready to give up. They believed that there was no way Germany could win the war. But one man stood alone in his belief that victory would finally come to his beloved German "fatherland." Adolf Hitler, the *Fuehrer*, the German dictator and absolute commander of all German armed forces, had a plan that he firmly believed would bring victory.

Deeply depressed following the successful Allied breakout from Normandy in July, Hitler searched for a solution. He dreamed of a bold counterattack that would defeat and divide the Allied armies threatening the West Wall of Germany. Finally, in a meeting with his top generals on September 16, 1944, he announced his decision.

An avid student of military history, Hitler recalled how the German hero Frederick the Great, when facing defeat, went on the attack and conquered greatly superior foes. Looking at a battle map of the situation in 1944, Hitler recognized the potential weakness in the Allied line in the Ardennes. He then recalled the great victories of 1940 as his panzer armies had driven through that same Ardennes Forest to force the British and French to the beaches of Dunkirk and defeat. In a flash, his brilliant mind conceived a plan.

German Counterattack Planned

Overnight, Hitler's attitude switched from one of despair to complete elation and confidence. Sweeping aside all

Some two million German troops and thousands of tanks and other heavy equipment were gathered in Germany ready to attack.

American troops in the Ardennes region were resting and rearming at quiet bases, unaware of the German attack that was about to be unleashed.

objections, he ordered General Alfred Jodl and his staff to develop a plan that would call for a blitzkrieg counterattack in November under cover of winter cold and rain. The attack would thrust through the weakened American forces in the Ardennes and on to Antwerp, creating a giant bulge in the Allied defenses.

Such an attack, if successful, would divide the American and British armies and cut off their supplies. The weakened Allied forces could then be driven back to the English Channel and the North Sea. Superior German forces would force an Allied withdrawal to Great Britain as they had done at Dunkirk in 1940. Hitler ordered his generals, working in complete secrecy, to prepare plans that would accomplish these goals.

Wacht am Rhein

Hitler called his plan *Wacht am Rhein* (Watch on the Rhine). The Rhine River, just 50 to 100 miles to the east of Germany's West Wall, was a natural barrier to further Allied advances. Hitler wanted to prevent any possibility of the Allies ever crossing the Rhine at any point. A major counterattack and victory could remove that threat once and for all.

Even though the German General Staff did not have great faith in Hitler's ambitious goals, they went to work on various plans. Under the leadership of General Jodl, five different plans were submitted to Hitler. They involved the buildup of some 30 highly trained and well-equipped panzer (tank) and grenadier (infantry) divisions. These would be massed along the West Wall near the Ardennes in complete secrecy.

General Jodl finally narrowed down his various plans, including one major plan that matched Hitler's theories. Three German panzer armies would attack through the Ardennes, cross the Meuse River and capture Antwerp.

Although reinforcements and supplies had been moving to the German front lines steadily for almost three months, no one but Hitler's personal staff knew of the final plans. Hitler announced his plan to only his top generals in late October. When Field Marshals Gerd von Rundstedt and Walther Model and their chiefs of staff were finally informed they were horrified. They felt that the plan was much too ambitious and would surely fail.

Instead they offered what was called the "Small Solution," which involved attacks around Aachen to drive back the entire northern end of the 400-mile-long Allied line. Hitler disagreed. It would not achieve his grand plan of splitting the Allies and cutting off their supplies.

He insisted on his "Large Solution," the counterattack through the Ardennes. In order to allow more time for preparation, he calculated that the attack should commence on December 10. Final plans and movement of supplies continued at full speed. All movement was done at night or under cover of bad weather. Allied air reconnaissance could not be allowed to discover what was happening. After minor delays, Hitler finally ordered the attack to begin on December 16.

An American soldier walks slowly down a road in the Ardennes Forest. The coming Battle of the Bulge was to disrupt this peaceful scene.

U.S. Forces in Ardennes Unprepared

On December 15, 1944, the American VIII Corps was thinly spread throughout the Ardennes. The two divisions that were closest to the front were resting and licking their wounds following the heavy fighting in the Huertgens Forest which had taken place in October. The 9th Division, an undermanned armored division, and the untried 106th Division, which had just arrived from the United States, were scattered throughout the rest of the area. Two other partial divisions were resting and being re-equipped.

Occasionally there were brief skirmishes between the Americans and the Germans. However, no major battles were underway. Some German prisoners had been taken who warned of massive buildup and preparations on the German side of the lines. No one paid attention. Some called the Ardennes Forest the "Ghost Front"—a cold, rainy area with little contact with the enemy. Both sides seemed to be simply watching and waiting.

Young American boys, many among the first 18-year-old soldiers drafted, looked out from their shelters at snow-covered trees and dreamed of home. But other more experienced troops were worried. Forward units of the 106th Division were already a short distance into Germany. Earlier, they had broken through the Siegfried Line's tank traps and were surrounded on three sides by rugged ground called the *Schnee Eifel* (Snow Mountains), which were filled with hidden pillboxes, barbed wire and concealed troops. Moreover, to the north and south of this area were big gaps in the American lines. Most of the Ardennes front was only partially protected by newly arrived and inexperienced troops. This had all the makings of a disaster waiting to happen.

Warnings Ignored

To the rear of the front lines in the Belgian towns of Bastogne and St. Vith and numerous small villages, life went on as if it were peacetime. The American troops rested, watched movies, trained and worked on their weapons. U.S.O. (United Service Organization) entertainment groups were putting on shows in some of the camps.

At the same time some commanders were not so complacent. Reports were coming in of the sound of roaring motors and the movement of troops on the German side of the lines. A woman who had seen large movements of German troops across the line was sent to headquarters to report the sightings. Yet General Troy Middleton, commander of the VII Corps, still was unconvinced.

At higher headquarters, General Hodges, commander of the 1st U.S. Army, was continually warned by his intelligence experts that an attack was about to take place in the Ardennes. There were even reports that German troops dressed as American troops were being trained to act as spies. These reports were ignored. At the even higher headquarters of General Bradley's 12th Army Group, these warnings were also ignored. Even General Eisenhower's intelligence staff predicted that the German army was weakening and could not sustain a major attack.

Cheerful German troops share cigarettes as they await the order to attack.

The night of December 15, in spite of all warnings, almost all Americans behind the lines, from army privates to generals, slept soundly in their quarters. But across the West Wall everyone was wide awake and ready for action, tensely awaiting the order to attack. Three completely equipped German panzer armies, 250,000 strong, were making final preparations for the attack.

Some 75,000 fresh troops supported by hundreds of Tiger and Panther tanks and big guns had been added to the panzer armies at the last minute. Three million gallons of gasoline had been delivered to the front with 2 million more in reserve. Every tank and truck was filled with fuel and loaded with ammunition and other equipment. And 15,000 tons of ammunition had been doled out to the attacking armies with an equal amount held in reserve. Everything was ready to launch the first attacks of Wacht am Rhein against the Ardennes at daylight on December 16, 1944. The Battle of the Bulge was about to begin.

Chapter 4

BATTLE
OF THE BULGE

The German attack opened at 5:30 A.M. with a tremendous rolling artillery barrage all along the 85-mile front. It lasted for 45 minutes. Mortars and short-range artillery blasted the front lines. Howitzers and heavy-caliber railway guns threw shells deep into Allied territory. Their targets were communications centers and headquarters units behind the lines. American casualties were heavy.

The goal of the German attack was to create confusion, and the initial massive bombardment did just that. The stunned American troops rolled out of their beds in a state of shock.

As Hitler had hoped and planned, the initial attacks were made under a heavy fog. Allied aircraft, kept on the ground, were unable to search out and attack the enemy, much less support the confused Allied troops. Once the artillery barrage had lifted, elements of the German 5th, 6th and 7th Panzer Armies, with their Panther and Tiger tanks leading the way, began their advance into the Ardennes. Panzer grenadiers followed close behind. Altogether 250,000 German troops were involved.

In some areas they moved forward rapidly, attacking and overrunning disorganized and retreating American troops. However, in other areas pockets of hastily organized and well-entrenched American units met the attackers with heavy fire, slowing the advance. Both sides began to suffer heavy losses.

German troops rushing across a Belgian road past ruined U.S. equipment as they carry out their well-planned attacks

The three panzer armies had been assigned the task of driving through the Ardennes. Their goal was to reach the Belgian seaport of Antwerp and cut the Allied forces in half. The British would be trapped to the north, cut off from the main American forces located to the south of Antwerp. This also would cut the Allied supply lines and, if successful, victorious German troops could drive the battered Allied forces into the English Channel.

The German panzers quickly drove as deep as 40 miles into the Ardennes, creating the huge "bulge" in the Allied lines from which the battle takes its name. Advance German panzer units had cut a huge triangle in the Allied lines along a 60-mile front. Not until the Allied high command realized late on the afternoon of December 16 that a major attack was taking place, did resistance stiffen and reinforced American units begin to fight back. By this time thousands of U.S. soldiers had become casualties or had been captured.

Peiper's Panzers and the Malmedy Massacre

S.S. Colonel Jochen Peiper, a young veteran of the Russian Front, led his panzer group deep into Allied territory early on December 16. The S.S. *(Schutzstaffel)* were the elite Nazi guard and the best trained units in the Wehrmacht (German Army). Peiper was headed for the Meuse River bridges and the city of Liege.

Overcoming one obstacle after another, he made rapid headway. He destroyed dozens of American units as his panzers advanced. By the 17th, Peiper's panzer group was racing toward the key crossroads at the town of Malmedy. If he could control that strongpoint, he could crack the Allied northern defenses and drive on toward Antwerp. Near Malmedy his blitzkrieg attack overran an American battalion not equipped with tanks and heavy armament. Coming under fire and unable to fight back against the stronger panzer unit, the Americans surrendered. Colonel Peiper and his tanks sped past and headed at full speed toward their objectives to the west.

One of Peiper's officers, not wanting to be saddled with prisoners, herded some 150 of the captured American soldiers into a nearby field. For reasons unknown, the prisoners were suddenly fired upon and 85 unarmed Americans

SS Colonel Jochen Peiper (left) was a 29-year-old soldier who was completely devoted to Adolf Hitler and the Nazi cause. A cruel and ruthless commander, he led one of the most successful German attacks into the Ardennes. His troops were responsible for the Malmedy massacre.

A U.S. Army graves registration unit checks the bodies of American soldiers killed by their German captors during the Battle of the Bulge.

died. A few of the prisoners escaped and word of the Malmedy massacre spread through the U.S. forces. This hardened American defensive efforts throughout the Ardennes.

Peiper's dramatic advances began to slow as he became short of fuel and was held back by traffic jams and snow-clogged roads. If he had been able to continue his high-speed advance and other advancing panzer units had been as aggressive, the outcome of the Battle of the Bulge might have been different. However, American resistance stiffened rapidly and soon they were counterattacking. Bloody and costly battles took place almost hourly with tremendous losses to the American forces. But by fighting back bravely, the U.S. forces stopped the German advances throughout most of the Ardennes. By December 22 the German advance had ground to a halt on all of the attack routes.

Colonel Skorzeny's Commandos

On October 21 Adolf Hitler had personally selected Otto Skorzeny to head a commando unit that would operate in a most unorthodox manner behind American lines. Skorzeny was a ruthless and renowned commando leader who had rescued the Italian dictator Mussolini after the surrender of the Italians. Hitler ordered the S.S. colonel, an ardent Nazi, to recruit English-speaking soldiers from throughout the German forces and equip them with American uniforms and arms or dress them as civilians. In other words, they were to act as spies and commit sabotage and create confusion among the American forces. Called the 150th Panzer Brigade, they were known by the code-name *Greif*.

As the Ardennes invasion began, Skorzeny's Greif units, using American jeeps and other American vehicles, spread out behind American lines. They cut telephone wires, gave false information to American troops and advanced farther into the Ardennes than any other German unit. It was even rumored that they planned to kidnap General Eisenhower. As a result, SHAEF (Supreme Headquarters Allied Expeditionary Forces) was placed under heavy security and the general was practically a prisoner in his own headquarters.

However, without the anticipated support of advancing panzer units, many of Skorzeny's commandos were soon discovered. Treated as spies, many of those captured were tried on the spot and executed. Although Skorzeny's commandos created confusion, all in all the mission was not a success. It was a wasteful and cowardly effort on the part of the German army and their leader, Adolf Hitler.

American tanks and other reinforcements were rushed into the Ardennes from both the north and the south to counterattack the German forces.

Allied Forces Counterattack on All Sides

On December 18, General Eisenhower called a meeting of his key commanders. They met with their commander in chief and received orders to halt the attacks on the German West Wall at all costs. Faced with the possible annihilation of the entire American Ardennes force, Eisenhower ordered all units to direct their efforts against the German advance in the Ardennes. General Patton had already turned his forces northward and had made contact with units of the 7th Panzer Army. The 1st U.S. Army under General Hodges, began to attack southward against the fast-moving 5th and 6th Panzer Armies.

Chapter 5

BASTOGNE UNDER SIEGE

Bastogne was a major city and strongpoint in the southeast section of the Ardennes. Seven major roads converged there. It was considered vital that the Germans capture it early, by the third day of the campaign. This network of highways was needed to supply the rapidly advancing German forces.

General Hasso von Manteuffel's 5th Panzer Army was attacking and capturing villages and American positions all around Bastogne. By December 19 it appeared that Bastogne itself would soon fall to vastly superior German forces. However, the Americans held on.

German forces advanced to within a few miles of the besieged city of Bastogne before being turned back.

An American mortar company fires on advancing German troops during the fight for Bastogne.

The German panzer army continued its attacks on Bastogne. By the 19th, German panzer and grenadier units were poised for a final assault on that key city. General Troy Middleton's U.S. Army VIII Corps, whose headquarters were in Bastogne, recognized the threat and set up strong defenses, repulsing the first attacks.

While Bastogne was successfully fighting off defeat and capture, German units had bypassed the city and advanced farther into the Ardennes. Outlying American forces were defeated with great losses. Attacks on Bastogne continued but were held off by reinforcements that began to arrive from General Patton's 3rd Army.

Meanwhile, other units of the 5th Panzer Army were preparing to attack Bastogne from the north and west. But still the Bastogne defenders fought back. At the same time the 101st Airborne Division from General Patton's 3rd Army, commanded by General Anthony McAuliffe, broke through the German lines from the south to reinforce the embattled city. A firm defensive line was soon set up all around Bastogne.

As the American defenses stiffened, the German attacks began to falter. Both sides were suffering heavy losses. Having failed to capture the city earlier, the Germans were now confronted by a strong American defense. By the 21st Bastogne was under a complete state of siege, but the key transportation hub was still controlled by American forces.

"Nuts" to Surrender Demand

Fortunately, the weather began to clear and Allied air power came into play. Supplies were dropped or flown in to the heavily engaged American troops. Allied fighters and bombers were at last able to bomb and strafe the attacking German panzers.

However, Bastogne was still under a complete state of siege. By this time General Anthony McAuliffe was in command in Bastogne and was coordinating its defense.

Standing in front of his headquarters in the city of Bastogne, General McAuliffe greets a fellow officer during the defense of that strategic city.

A battalion of U.S. Army 155mm howitzers fire on the enemy as the defeated German army begins its retreat toward the Rhine River.

Thinking he had the battle for Bastogne won, General Heinz Kokott, commander of the 26th *Volksgrenadiers*, asked the Americans to surrender. General McAuliffe responded with his famous reply—"Nuts!" This was indicative of the high level of morale and the will to win held by American troops during this crucial battle. Bastogne continued to fight off its attackers.

On Christmas Day the fate of Bastogne was still in question. General Kokott launched another major offensive only to fall into a well-laid trap. A major part of the attacking German troops was wiped out in an ambush laid by a U.S. parachute infantry battalion and a tank destroyer battalion. As more U.S. reinforcements arrived from the south, the far-ranging German panzer armies began to withdraw. On December 26, tanks from General Patton's 3rd Army broke through the German lines and joined up with General McAuliffe's forces in Bastogne. The siege was over.

Chapter 6

NORDWIND and BODENPLATTE

Although the German panzers had come to within a few miles of the Meuse River at the town of Dinant, they had never been able to cross it as planned. From December 26, following the relief of Bastogne, the advance of the German panzer armies had been stopped. The Allied forces had set up solid defense lines surrounding the entire "bulge" and were on the offensive.

Hitler, anticipating the need for additional forces, either to support a victorious advance to Antwerp or to take pressure off a losing situation, had two plans. They were put into effect on December 31, 1944, and January 1, 1945.

Operation Nordwind

The first plan, called *Nordwind* (North Wind), was to take the pressure off the retreating German troops in the Ardennes. This plan involved another major offensive, this time by the German Army Group G under the command of General Herman Balck. About 60 miles to the south of Bastogne, Operation Nordwind was put into effect to invade the Alsace region of France and to draw American troops away from battles the Germans were losing in the Ardennes.

On December 31 General Balck's forces attacked across the West Wall into the Alsace-Lorraine section of France. There he was met by the U.S. 6th Army Group commanded by General Jacob L. Devers and the French 1st Army. Although the 6th Army had been weakened by the fact that

American infantrymen firing across an open field in the Ardennes as they pursue the retreating German army

many of its troops had been sent north to fight in the Ardennes, General Devers was well prepared. He had excellent intelligence concerning the enemy's movements and was ready when the attack started.

Following a plan prepared by General Eisenhower's headquarters, the U.S. 7th Army commanded by General Alexander M. Patch was to withdraw before the enemy attack. This would straighten and strengthen the Allied line of defense. However, this would also mean the loss of the famous old French city of Strasbourg. This proposed action infuriated General Charles de Gaulle, commander of the Free French forces in France. In direct violation of military orders he sent a French army to defend Strasbourg.

Finally, to prevent a serious breach between the Americans and the French, General Eisenhower agreed to change plans. The French would defend Strasbourg and U.S. forces would defend the balance of the line to the north.

Nordwind had been a failure as far as the Germans were concerned. They made only small gains and suffered heavy losses. It finally drew to a close in late January when Hitler had to transfer three divisions to the Eastern front to fight new attacks by the Russians. It had no effect on the final victory by the Americans in the Ardennes.

Operation Bodenplatte

With the Wehrmacht failing on the ground, Hitler decided to call on the Luftwaffe (German air force) to strike a major blow in an attempt to cripple the Allied air forces that were doing such great damage. He created the plan for Operation *Bodenplatte* (Ground Slam) as a last ditch effort to turn the tide in the Ardennes.

Early on New Year's Day 1945, a giant Luftwaffe force, Jagdkorps II, executed a superbly planned action. Some 1,000 Messerschmitt 109 and Focke Wulf 190 fighter-bombers delivered a carefully planned attack against the airfields in Holland and Belgium that were providing the air-ground support and airborne supply for the American armies in the Battle of the Bulge. Some called this mission the "Hangover Raid" because the Germans planned to attack when American troops were waking up after New Year's Eve parties on Allied bases.

An American anti-aircraft gun crew observe the giant air battle taking place over Allied air bases during Operation Bodenplatte.

In one respect the mission was successful. It destroyed more than 350 Allied aircraft and damaged many more. On the other hand the mission was even more costly for the Luftwaffe. They lost some 300 aircraft and almost an equal number of pilots were killed or captured. The Allies could replace their aircraft and pilots within a few weeks. The Germans not only could not replace their aircraft, but more important, they could not replace their pilots. The Luftwaffe never recovered from these terrible losses.

Hitler's Weather

While Hitler's elaborate plans were failing, one enemy was defeating both Allies and Germans alike—winter. The weather in the Ardennes was predictable in that it was usually bad from November on. Heavy fog and rain were present most of December as the Germans planned and executed the Wacht am Rhein campaign. And when winter weather really set in in late December and January, both sides had to contend with deep snow and bitter cold.

The weather during the early battles in the Ardennes could be called "Hitler's weather." The entire German strategy was built around the fact that weather would keep Allied planes on the ground, slow down reinforcements, and generally disrupt all military operations. However, in the long run the weather slowed the German advances as well, as they tried to negotiate slippery roads and the muddy terrain of the Ardennes Forest.

In the rugged hills surrounding Bastogne, freezing weather can occur through almost half the year. In January the snowfall can exceed a foot in a single day with deep drifts that bring traffic to a standstill.

Luck was with Hitler when the attack was launched on December 16. Bad weather held for eight days and kept Allied air support grounded. At the same time, though, rising temperatures brought thaws that turned the frozen roads to mud and created havoc for both sides.

American troops form a chow line in frigid winter weather as the Battle of the Bulge draws to a close.

As many as 4,000 Allied aircraft were poised for attack from airfields in Scotland, Belgium and the Netherlands. Day after day they were kept on the ground by the heavy fog and rain. Finally on December 23, a so-called "Russian high" brought cold, clear weather from the north. "Hitler weather" had changed and the skies were clear over the entire Ardennes. The Allied air forces went to work. The good weather continued for four days, giving them a chance to batter the German panzers and motorized troops stuck in the deep snow as they struggled toward the front.

One recurring theme for both sides was "we are fighting the weather as much as the enemy." Everyone suffered. While "Hitler's weather" gave the German armies a good start in their attempts to reach the Meuse River on the road to Antwerp, it soon turned against them. And the ill-equipped Americans suffered from the cold so that cases of frozen feet were as numerous as battle casualties.

In the long run, though, American military superiority and more favorable weather turned the tide in the Allies' favor. By the end of January 1945 the Ardennes was clear of German invaders and the Allies were again advancing toward the Rhine river. The German Watch on the Rhine campaign and the Battle of the Bulge had ended.

Chapter 7

THE BRIDGE AT REMAGEN

The German counteroffensive in the Ardennes had caused a temporary delay for the Allies but had finally failed. By mid-January all of the Nazi forces in the Ardennes were in full retreat and were being driven back toward the Rhine River. General Eisenhower reconfirmed his plan to continue his "broad front" strategy with the main target being the Ruhr Valley, the industrial heart of Germany.

On January 3, Field Marshal Montgomery's forces along with the U.S. 7th Army began attacking the Ardennes from the north. Joining up with U.S. 3rd Army units advancing from the south, these two forces cut off and captured thousands of German troops. By January 10 Hitler at last was convinced that the Ardennes counteroffensive had failed and ordered the withdrawal of all German troops to behind the West Wall. On the next day alone some 15,000 Germans were trapped and captured as more Allied forces moved into action. Retreating in complete chaos and under continuous Allied attacks, the German withdrawal from the Ardennes was completed by January 22.

The Rhineland Campaign

With the Battle of the Bulge behind them, Allied forces all up and down the West Wall were ready to continue their march to the Rhine. On the other side of the Wall, in Germany, Hitler was determined to prevent the Allies from reaching the Rhine. This giant waterway was a natural barrier and it was also a key supply line for both German military and industry.

The Allied strategy called for a massive offensive in the north and steady pressure on the entire frontier to keep the faltering German armies engaged on all fronts. Field Marshal Montgomery's 21st Army Group, reinforced by the U.S. 9th Army, first attacked on January 15 when General Dempsey's 2nd British Army won decisive victories. This was followed in February by major drives into the Ruhr Valley.

Operations Veritable, Grenade, and Blockbuster

General Sir Henry Crerar and the 1st Canadian Army led these drives by launching Operation Veritable on February 8. Preceded by a heavy bombardment from over 1,000 guns, the attack went well as the Canadians surged past the West Wall and into Germany. They rolled right over weak German defenses, inflicting heavy casualties and capturing some 1,300 German soldiers. The advance was soon brought to a halt by new German reinforcements. The Canadians, however, having engaged in bitter fighting, had accomplished a sizeable advance.

Lieutenant General William H. Simpson and the U.S. 9th Army launched Operation Grenade on February 23. Fighting through flood waters from Roer River dams destroyed by the Germans, they made good progress since much of the defending panzers and grenadiers had been drawn north to fight off the Canadians. On that same date, attacking from the southern portion of the U.S. lines, General Hodges's 1st Army also breached the West Wall and began a rapid advance toward the key city of Cologne on the Rhine.

Another Canadian force launched Operation Blockbuster on February 26. Along with General Crerar's forces they advanced even closer to the Rhine near the major German city of Wesel. The three pincer-like operations all met with considerable success. By the first week in March they were on the western banks of the Rhine.

American troops and equipment successfully crossed the Rhine River after capturing the bridge at Remagen, Germany.

German Southern Defenses Collapse

Meanwhile, after clearing the German threat in the Ardennes, General Patton's 3rd Army went on the attack through the snow-covered hills of the Eifel area in Germany. They too were rapidly approaching the Rhine. Still farther to the south General Patch's 7th Army unleashed Operation Undertone and moved rapidly across the West Wall into Germany in that area. The French 1st Army was also successful at the extreme southern end of the Allied lines as they cleaned up a German-held area called the Colmar pocket and began their advance toward German territory.

This beautiful memorial was erected in the Ardennes Forest by the citizens of Belgium in honor of the Allied soldiers who had died during the Battle of the Bulge.

St. Nicholas rides on a weapon's carrier as British troops bring food and gifts to the children of the Netherlands. The war had finally ended for this battle-scarred country.

GLOSSARY

Allies The nations that joined together during World War II to defeat Germany, Japan and Italy: France, Great Britain, China, the Soviet Union and the United States.

Ardennes Forest A large wooded area in southeastern Belgium in which the Battle of the Bulge took place.

blitzkrieg Means "lightning war" in German.

commando A soldier specially trained to make sudden destructive raids against an enemy.

glider An engineless aircraft that is designed to fly using air currents after being towed aloft by an airplane.

grenadier A German infantryman.

howitzer A large cannon used for long-range artillery bombardment.

Luftwaffe The German air force before and during World War II.

Nazi A person or idea belonging to the German National Socialist party.

panzer A German tank.

paratroops Soldiers trained to jump from aircraft using parachutes.

pillbox A small reinforced concrete structure used to house machine guns or other weapons.

pontoon bridge A temporary floating bridge using rubber inflatable rafts or other craft for support.

S.S. Abbreviation for Schutzstaffel. Elite German army units made up of members of the Nazi party loyal to Adolf Hitler. They were the best trained troops in the German army.

Wehrmacht The German army.

INDEX

Aachen, Germany 11, 13, 16, 20
Allied forces 7, 8, 9, 11, 34, 39
Alsace-Lorraine, France 34
Antwerp, Belgium 10, 12, 13, 19, 20, 25, 34, 38
Ardennes Forest 7, 10, 11, 14, 16, 17, 20, 21, 25, 27, 30, 34, 35, 37, 38, 39, 43, 44
Arnhem, Netherland 10, 11, 12

Balck, General Herman 34
Bastogne, Belgium 22, 30, 31, 32, 33, 34, 37
Belgium 8, 10, 11, 36, 38
Berlin, Germany 11, 42
blitzkrieg attacks 11, 19, 26
Bradley, General 22
British forces 5, 8, 12, 40, 43

Canada 40
Canadian forces 5, 12, 40
Charlemagne 13
Cherbourg, France 9
Colmar pocket 41
Cologne 40
Crerar, General Sir Henry 40

D-Day 5
de Gaulle, General Charles 35
Dempsey, General 40
Devers, General Jacob L. 34, 35
Dinant, Belgium 34
Dunkirk, France 17, 19

Eifel area, Germany 41
Eisenhower, General Dwight D. 9, 10, 12, 14, 22, 29, 35, 39
English Channel 19, 25

Focke Wulf 190 fighter-bombers 36

France 7, 8, 43
Frederick the Great 17
French forces 34, 41
Frost, Major John Dutton 9

Germany 7, 8, 11, 39, 40
Ghost Front (Ardennes Forest) 21

Hangover Raid 36
Hitler, Adolf 7, 17, 19, 20, 24, 29, 34, 35, 36, 37, 39, 42, 43
Hodge, General Courtney H. 8, 13, 22, 29, 40, 42
Holland 10, 36
Huertgen Forest 13, 14, 21

Jodl, General Alfred 19, 20, 42

Kokott, General Heinz 33

Large Solution 20
Luftwaffe 36, 37
Luxembourg 11

Maginot Line 14, 16
Malmedy massacre 26, 27
McAuliffe, General Anthony 31, 32, 33
Messerschmitt 109 36
Meuse River 20, 26, 34, 38
Middleton, General Troy 22, 31
Model, Field Marshal Walther 20
Montgomery, Field Marshal Bernard 8, 10, 11, 12, 14, 39, 40

Nazi armies 5
Netherlands 9, 13, 38
Normandy 7, 8, 9, 17, 42
North Sea 12, 19

101st Airborne Division 10, 31
106th Division 21, 22
Operation Blockbuster 40
Operation Bodenplatte (Ground
   Slam) 36
Operation Cobra 6
Operation Dragoon 6
Operation Grenade 40
Operation Market-Garden 8, 10,
   11
Operation Nordwind (North Wind)
   34, 35
Operation Overlord 5
Operation Undertone 41
Operation Veritable 40
Our River 11

Panther tanks 23, 24
Panzer Army 29, 30, 31
Paris, France 8
Patch, General Alexander M. 35,
   41
Patton, General George S. 8, 14,
   16, 29, 31, 33, 41
Peiper, S.S. Colonel Jochen 26

Ramsay, Admiral Sir Bertram 12
Red-Ball Express 7
Remagen Bridge, Remagen,
   Germany 41, 42
Rhine River 10, 19, 33, 38, 39, 41,
   42
Rhineland Campaign 39, 42
Roer River 14, 40
Roer Valley 14
Rotterdam, Netherlands 10
Ruhr Valley, Germany 13, 39, 40
Russia 8, 35, 43

S.S. (Schutzstaffel) 26
Saar region 14
St. Vith, Belgium 22
Scheldt waterway 10, 12, 13
Schnee Eifel (Snow Mountains)
   22
Scotland 38
SHAEF (Supreme Headquarters
   Allied Expeditionary Forces)
   29
Siegfried Line 11, 22
Simpson, Lieutenant General
   William H. 14, 40
Skorzeny, Colonel Otto 28, 29
Small Solution 20
Speer, Albert 42
Strasbourg, France 35
Switzerland 9, 10

Tiger tanks 23, 24
26th Volksgrenadiers 33

U.S. forces 7, 8, 10, 11, 13, 14, 21,
   22, 27, 29, 31, 33, 34, 35, 39,
   40, 41, 42
U.S.O. (United Service Organization) 22
United States 43

V-2 rockets 42
Verdun, France 8
von Manteuffel, General Hasso
   30
von Rundstedt, Field Marshal
   Gerd 20

Wacht am Rhein 19, 23, 37, 43
Wehrmacht 24, 25, 26, 29, 30, 34,
   36, 38
Wesel, Germany 40